THE BUSY ENTREPRENUER'S
Gratitude
JOURNAL

Ignite your gratitude!

Bonn S—

BONNI GOLDBERG
VIZYE PUBLICATIONS
PORTLAND, OR

Published by Vizye Publications in 2017
First edition; First printing

Design and writing © 2017 Bonni Goldberg
Cover by Kayla Himmelberger

ISBN 978-0-9967524-3-5

Dedication

To the Teachers:
Lou Dalo
Tim Grahl
Danny Iny
Kristen Joy Laidig

Introduction

Gratitude is riches. Complaint is poverty.
Doris Day

Spiritual traditions have always taught that gratitude improves our lives. Now there's more and more evidence coming from neuroscience, leadership, and positive psychology studies that demonstrate the impact of a gratitude habit on success.

The journey as an entrepreneur includes snags, frustrations, disappointments and rejection. Too often these moments drain energy, eat away at determination and deflate confidence unless you have the right tool to manage them. Successful entrepreneurs will tell you that gratitude is essential.

As a busy entrepreneur it's also essential to spend your time, money and energy wisely. Invest just two minutes a day in this specially designed journal to make gratitude a habit and gain the following benefits:

- increase your energy level
- help you network
- increase your decision making capabilities
- increase your productivity
- stay positive and focused
- reduce envious feelings
- bounce back from stress and disappointment more quickly
- improve sleep
- help you get mentors
- increase your long-term well-being over 10%—the same impact as doubling your income

Social entrepreneur and Nobel Peace Prize winner, Muhammad Yunus says, "All human beings are born entrepreneurs. Some get a chance to unleash that capacity. Some never got the chance, never knew that he or she has that capacity." Start with gratitude that you're unleashing your unique contribution. Discover the power of gratitude in the pages of this journal.

*The critical thing is whether you take things
for granted or take them with gratitude.*
Gilbert K. Chesterton

i

Table of Contents

Gratitude
Daily & Weekly

Develop an attitude of gratitude, and give thanks for everything that happens to you, knowing that every step forward is a step toward achieving something bigger and better than your current situation.
Brian Tracy

Gratitude is the healthiest of all human emotions. The more you express gratitude for what you have, the more likely you will have even more to express gratitude for.
Naveen Jain

In this section, every day write down one thing you're grateful for in each of the following three categories:

 Your work as an entrepreneur today. This could be something you did, something that happened, something you realized or learned. It can also be something you didn't do or that didn't happen.

 Yourself. In this category, you can focus on an aspect of your personality, an ability, a relationship you have, an event, a place, an experience, a compliment you received — anything that has to do with you and your life today.

 The world around you. This final category can be something in nature, something you've read or heard about today, something you've observed. One way to focus on the world around you is to think in terms of your senses — what have you seen, heard, tasted, smelled, touched or felt that you're grateful for?

At the end of the week, take a minute to review and reflect on what you've written each day that week and use the Week's Review to record what you noticed.

Date: _____

Work _____

Self _____

World _____

Date: _____

Work _____

Self _____

World _____

Date: _____

Work _____

Self _____

World _____

Date: _____

Work _____

Self _____

World _____

Date: _____

Work

_____

Self

_____

World

_____

Date: _____

Work

_____

Self

_____

World

_____

Date: _____

Work _____

Self _____

World _____

Overall Week's Gratitude

Work _____

Self _____

World _____

Date: _____

Work

_____

Self

_____

World

_____

Date: _____

Work

_____

Self

_____

World

_____

Date: _____

Work _____

Self _____

World _____

Date: _____

Work _____

Self _____

World _____

Date: _____

Work

_____

Self

_____

World

_____

Work

_____

Date: _____

Self

_____

World

_____

Date: _____

Work

_____

Self

_____

World

_____

Overall Week's Gratitude

Work

_____

Self

_____

World

_____

Date: _____

Work _____

Self _____

World _____

Date: _____

Work _____

Self _____

World _____

Date: _____

Work

_____

Self

_____

World

_____

Date: _____

Work

_____

Self

_____

World

_____

Date: _____

Work _____

Self _____

World _____

Date: _____

Work _____

Self _____

World _____

Date: _____

Work _____

Self _____

World _____

Overall Week's Gratitude

Work _____

Self _____

World _____

Date: _____

Work _____

Self _____

World _____

Date: _____

Work _____

Self _____

World _____

Date: _____

Work _____

Self _____

World _____

Date: _____

Work _____

Self _____

World _____

Date: _____

Work
_____

Self
_____

World
_____

Date: _____

Work
_____

Self
_____

World
_____

Date: _____

Work

_____

Self

_____

World

Overall Week's Gratitude

Work

_____

Self

_____

World

_____

Date: _____

Work

_____

Self

_____

World

_____

Date: _____

Work

_____

Self

_____

World

_____

Date: _____

Work

_____

Self

_____

World

_____

Date: _____

Work

_____

Self

_____

World

_____

Date: _____

Work _____

Self _____

World _____

Date: _____

Work _____

Self _____

World _____

21

Date: _____

Work

_____

Self

_____

World

_____

Overall Week's Gratitude

Work

_____

Self

_____

World

_____

Date: _____

Work _____

Self _____

World _____

Date: _____

Work _____

Self _____

World _____

Date: _____

Work _____

Self _____

World _____

Date: _____

Work _____

Self _____

World _____

Date: _____

Work

_____

Self

_____

World

_____

Date: _____

Work

_____

Self

_____

World

_____

Date: _____

Work _____

Self _____

World _____

Overall Week's Gratitude

Work _____

Self _____

World _____

Date: _____

Work _____

Self _____

World _____

Date: _____

Work _____

Self _____

World _____

Date: _____

Work _____

Self _____

World _____

Date: _____

Work _____

Self _____

World _____

Date: _____

Work _____

Self _____

World _____

Date: _____

Work _____

Self _____

World _____

Date: _____

Work _____

Self _____

World _____

Overall Week's Gratitude

Work _____

Self _____

World _____

Date: _____

Work

_____

Self

_____

World

_____

Date: _____

Work

_____

Self

_____

World

Date: _____

Work _____

Self _____

World _____

Date: _____

Work _____

Self _____

World _____

Date: _____

Work _____

Self _____

World _____

Date: _____

Work _____

Self _____

World _____

Date: _____

Work

_____

Self

_____

World

_____

Overall Week's Gratitude

Work

_____

Self

_____

World

_____

Date: _____

Work

_____

Self

_____

World

_____

Date: _____

Work

_____

Self

_____

World

_____

35

Date: _____

Work _____

Self _____

World _____

Date: _____

Work _____

Self _____

World _____

Date: _____

Work

_____

Self

_____

World

_____

Date: _____

Work

_____

Self

_____

World

_____

37

Date: _____

Work _____

Self _____

World _____

Overall Week's Gratitude

Work _____

Self _____

World _____

Date: _____

Work _____

Self _____

World _____

Date: _____

Work _____

Self _____

World _____

Date: _____

Work
_____

Self
_____

World
_____

Date: _____

Work
_____

Self
_____

World
_____

Date: _____

Work

_____

Self

_____

World

Date: _____

Work

_____

Self

_____

World

_____

Date: _____

Work _____

Self _____

World _____

Overall Week's Gratitude

Work _____

Self _____

World _____

Date: _____

Work

_____

Self

_____

World

_____

━━━━━━━━━━━━━━━━━━━━━━━━━━━━━━━━━━━━━

Date: _____

Work

_____

Self

_____

World

_____

Date: _____

Work _____

Self _____

World _____

Date: _____

Work _____

Self _____

World _____

44

Date: _____

Work

_____

Self

_____

World

_____

Date: _____

Work

_____

Self

_____

World

_____

Date: _____

Work _____

Self _____

World _____

Overall Week's Gratitude

Work _____

Self _____

World _____

Date: _____

Work _____

Self _____

World _____

Date: _____

Work _____

Self _____

World _____

47

Date: _____

Work

_____

Self

_____

World

_____

Date: _____

Work

_____

Self

_____

World

_____

Date: _____

Work

_____

Self

_____

World

_____

Date: _____

Work

_____

Self

_____

World

_____

Date: _____

Work
_____

Self
_____

World
_____

Overall Week's Gratitude

Work
_____

Self
_____

World
_____

Date: _____

Work
_____

Self
_____

World
_____

Date: _____

Work
_____

Self
_____

World
_____

Date: _____

Work _____

Self _____

World _____

Date: _____

Work _____

Self _____

World _____

Date: _____

Work _____

Self _____

World _____

Date: _____

Work _____

Self _____

World _____

Date: _____

Work _____

Self _____

World _____

Overall Week's Gratitude

Work _____

Self _____

World _____

Date: _____

Work _____

Self _____

World _____

Date: _____

Work _____

Self _____

World _____

55

Date: _____

Work _____

Self _____

World _____

Date: _____

Work _____

Self _____

World _____

Date: _____

Work _____

Self _____

World _____

Date: _____

Work _____

Self _____

World _____

Date: _____

Work _____

Self _____

World _____

Overall Week's Gratitude

Work _____

Self _____

World _____

Date: _____

Work _____

Self _____

World _____

Date: _____

Work _____

Self _____

World _____

Date: _____

Work _____

Self _____

World _____

Date: _____

Work _____

Self _____

World _____

Date: _____

Work _____

Self _____

World _____

Date: _____

Work _____

Self _____

World _____

Date: _____

Work

_____

Self

_____

World

Overall Week's Gratitude

Work

_____

Self

_____

World

Date: _____

Work _____

Self _____

World _____

Date: _____

Work _____

Self _____

World _____

Date: _____

Work

_____

Self

_____

World

_____

Date: _____

Work

_____

Self

_____

World

_____

Date: _____

Work
_____

Self
_____

World
_____

Date: _____

Work
_____

Self
_____

World
_____

Date: _____

Work

_____

Self

_____

World

_____

Overall Week's Gratitude

Work

_____

Self

_____

World

_____

Date: _____

Work _____

Self _____

World _____

Date: _____

Work _____

Self _____

World _____

Date: _____

Work

_____

Self

_____

World

_____

Date: _____

Work

_____

Self

_____

World

_____

Date: _____

Work _____

Self _____

World _____

Date: _____

Work _____

Self _____

World _____

Date: _____

Work

_____

Self

_____

World

Overall Week's Gratitude

Work

_____

Self

_____

World

Date: _____

Work

_____

Self

_____

World

_____

Date: _____

Work

_____

Self

_____

World

Date: _____

Work

_____

Self

_____

World

_____

Date: _____

Work

_____

Self

_____

World

_____

Date: _____

Work _____

Self _____

World _____

Date: _____

Work _____

Self _____

World _____

73

Date: _____

Work
_____

Self
_____

World
_____

Overall Week's Gratitude

Work
_____

Self
_____

World
_____

Date: _____

Work _____

Self _____

World _____

Date: _____

Work _____

Self _____

World _____

Date: _____

Work

_____

Self

_____

World

_____

Date: _____

Work

_____

Self

_____

World

_____

Date: _____

Work _____

Self _____

World _____

Date: _____

Work _____

Self _____

World _____

77

Date: _____

Work

_____

Self

_____

World

_____

Overall Week's Gratitude

Work

_____

Self

_____

World

_____

Date: _____

Work _____

Self _____

World _____

Date: _____

Work _____

Self _____

World _____

Date: _____

Work _____

Self _____

World _____

Date: _____

Work _____

Self _____

World _____

Date: _____

Work _____

Self _____

World _____

Date: _____

Work _____

Self _____

World _____

81

Date: _____

Work

_____

Self

_____

World

_____

Overall Week's Gratitude

Work

_____

Self

_____

World

_____

Date: _____

Work
_____

Self
_____

World
_____

Date: _____

Work
_____

Self
_____

World
_____

Date: _____

Work

_____

Self

_____

World

_____

Date: _____

Work

_____

Self

_____

World

_____

Date: _____

Work _____

Self _____

World _____

Date: _____

Work _____

Self _____

World _____

Date: _____

Work _____

Self _____

World _____

Overall Week's Gratitude

Work _____

Self _____

World _____

Date: _____

Work _____

Self _____

World _____

Date: _____

Work _____

Self _____

World _____

Date: _____

Work
_____

Self
_____

World
_____

Date: _____

Work
_____

Self
_____

World
_____

Date: _____

Work
_____

Self
_____

World
_____

Date: _____

Work
_____

Self
_____

World
_____

Date: _____

Work

_____

Self

_____

World

_____

Overall Week's Gratitude

Work

_____

Self

_____

World

_____

Date: _____

Work _____

Self _____

World _____

Date: _____

Work _____

Self _____

World _____

Date: _____

Work
_____

Self
_____

World
_____

Date: _____

Work
_____

Self
_____

World
_____

Date: _____

Work
_____

Self
_____

World
_____

Date: _____

Work
_____

Self
_____

World
_____

93

Date: _____

Work _____

Self _____

World _____

Overall Week's Gratitude

Work _____

Self _____

World _____

Date: _____

Work
_____

Self
_____

World
_____

Date: _____

Work
_____

Self
_____

World
_____

Date: _____

Work _____

Self _____

World _____

Date: _____

Work _____

Self _____

World _____

Date: _____

Work _____

Self _____

World _____

Date: _____

Work _____

Self _____

World _____

Date: _____

Work _____

Self _____

World _____

Overall Week's Gratitude

Work _____

Self _____

World _____

Date: _____

Work _____

Self _____

World _____

Date: _____

Work _____

Self _____

World _____

Date: _____

Work

_____

Self

_____

World

_____

Date: _____

Work

_____

Self

_____

World

_____

Date: _____

Work
_____

Self
_____

World
_____

Date: _____

Work
_____

Self
_____

World
_____

Date: _____

Work _____

Self _____

World _____

Overall Week's Gratitude

Work _____

Self _____

World _____

Date: _____

Work _____

Self _____

World _____

Date: _____

Work _____

Self _____

World _____

Date: _____

Work _____

Self _____

World _____

Date: _____

Work _____

Self _____

World _____

Date: _____

Work _____

Self _____

World _____

Date: _____

Work _____

Self _____

World _____

Date: _____

Work _____

Self _____

World _____

Overall Week's Gratitude

Work _____

Self _____

World _____

Date: _____

Work _____

Self _____

World _____

Date: _____

Work _____

Self _____

World _____

Date: _____

Work _____

Self _____

World _____

Date: _____

Work _____

Self _____

World _____

Date: _____

Work _____

Self _____

World _____

Date: _____

Work _____

Self _____

World _____

Date: _____

Work

_____

Self

_____

World

_____

Overall Week's Gratitude

Work

_____

Self

_____

World

_____

Date: _____

Work _____

Self _____

World _____

Date: _____

Work _____

Self _____

World _____

Date: _____

Work _____

Self _____

World _____

Date: _____

Work _____

Self _____

World _____

Date: _____

Work _____

Self _____

World _____

Date: _____

Work _____

Self _____

World _____

Date: _____

Work

_____

Self

_____

World

_____

Overall Week's Gratitude

Work

_____

Self

_____

World

_____

Date: _____

Work

_____

Self

_____

World

_____

Date: _____

Work

_____

Self

_____

World

_____

Date: _____

Work
_____

Self
_____

World
_____

Date: _____

Work
_____

Self
_____

World
_____

116

Date: _____

Work

_____

Self

_____

World

_____

Date: _____

Work

_____

Self

_____

World

_____

Date: _____

Work _____

Self _____

World _____

Overall Week's Gratitude

Work _____

Self _____

World _____

Date: _____

Work
_____

Self
_____

World
_____

Date: _____

Work
_____

Self
_____

World
_____

Date: _____

Work

_____

Self

_____

World

_____

Date: _____

Work

_____

Self

_____

World

_____

Date: _____

Work _____

Self _____

World _____

Date: _____

Work _____

Self _____

World _____

Date: _____

Work

_____

Self

_____

World

Overall Week's Gratitude

Work

_____

Self

_____

World

_____

Date: _____

Work _____

Self _____

World _____

Date: _____

Work _____

Self _____

World _____

Date: _____

Work _____

Self _____

World _____

Date: _____

Work _____

Self _____

World _____

Date: _____

Work _____

Self _____

World _____

Date: _____

Work _____

Self _____

World _____

Date: _____

Work _____

Self _____

World _____

Overall Week's Gratitude

Work _____

Self _____

World _____

Date: _____

Work

_____

Self

_____

World

_____

Date: _____

Work

_____

Self

_____

World

_____

127

Date: _____

Work
_____

Self
_____

World
_____

Date: _____

Work
_____

Self
_____

World
_____

Date: _____

Work

_____

Self

_____

World

_____

Date: _____

Work

_____

Self

_____

World

Date: _____

Work _____

Self _____

World _____

Overall Week's Gratitude

Work _____

Self _____

World _____

Date: _____

Work _____

Self _____

World _____

Date: _____

Work _____

Self _____

World _____

Date: _____

Work

Self

World

World

Date: _____

Work

Self

World

Date: _____

Work
_____

Self
_____

World
_____

Date: _____

Work
_____

Self
_____

World
_____

Date: _____

Work _____

Self _____

World _____

Overall Week's Gratitude

Work _____

Self _____

World _____

Date: _____

Work _____

Self _____

World _____

Date: _____

Work _____

Self _____

World _____

Date: _____

Work _____

Self _____

World _____

Date: _____

Work _____

Self _____

World _____

Date: _____

Work _____

Self _____

World _____

Date: _____

Work _____

Self _____

World _____

Date: _____

Work _____

Self _____

World _____

Overall Week's Gratitude

Work _____

Self _____

World _____

Date: _____

Work
_____

Self
_____

World
_____

Date: _____

Work
_____

Self
_____

World
_____

Date: _____

Work _____

Self _____

World _____

Date: _____

Work _____

Self _____

World _____

Date: _____

Work
_____

Self
_____

World
_____

Date: _____

Work
_____

Self
_____

World
_____

Date: _____

Work
_____

Self
_____

World
_____

Overall Week's Gratitude

Work
_____

Self
_____

World
_____

Date: _____

Work

_____

Self

_____

World

_____

Date: _____

Work

_____

Self

_____

World

_____

Date: _____

Work

_____

Self

_____

World

_____

Date: _____

Work

_____

Self

_____

World

_____

Date: _____

Work _____

Self _____

World _____

Date: _____

Work _____

Self _____

World _____

Date: _____

Work _____

Self _____

World _____

Overall Week's Gratitude

Work _____

Self _____

World _____

Date: _____

Work _____

Self _____

World _____

Date: _____

Work _____

Self _____

World _____

Date: _____

Work _____

Self _____

World _____

Date: _____

Work _____

Self _____

World _____

Date: _____

Work

_____

Self

_____

World

_____

Date: _____

Work

_____

Self

_____

World

_____

Date: _____

Work _____

Self _____

World _____

Overall Week's Gratitude

Work _____

Self _____

World _____

Date: _____

Work _____

Self _____

World _____

Date: _____

Work _____

Self _____

World _____

Date: _____

Work
_____

Self
_____

World
_____

Date: _____

Work
_____

Self
_____

World
_____

Date: _____

Work _____

Self _____

World _____

Date: _____

Work _____

Self _____

World _____

Date: _____

Work

_____

Self

_____

World

_____

Overall Week's Gratitude

Work

_____

Self

_____

World

_____

Date: _____

Work _____

Self _____

World _____

Date: _____

Work _____

Self _____

World _____

Date: _____

Work _____

Self _____

World _____

Date: _____

Work _____

Self _____

World _____

Date: _____

Work

_____

Self

_____

World

_____

Date: _____

Work

_____

Self

_____

World

_____

157

Date: _____

Work

_____

Self

_____

World

Overall Week's Gratitude

Work

_____

Self

_____

World

Date: _____

Work
_____

Self
_____

World
_____

Date: _____

Work
_____

Self
_____

World
_____

Date: _____

Work _____

Self _____

World _____

Date: _____

Work _____

Self _____

World _____

160

Date: _____

Work

_____

Self

_____

World

_____

Date: _____

Work

_____

Self

_____

World

_____

Date: _____

Work

_____

Self

_____

World

_____

Overall Week's Gratitude

Work

_____

Self

_____

World

_____

Date: _____

Work

_____

Self

_____

World

Date: _____

Work

_____

Self

_____

World

Date: _____

Work _____

Self _____

World _____

Date: _____

Work _____

Self _____

World _____

164

Date: _____

Work _____

Self _____

World _____

Date: _____

Work _____

Self _____

World _____

Date: _____

Work _____

Self _____

World _____

Overall Week's Gratitude

Work _____

Self _____

World _____

Date: _____

Work _____

Self _____

World _____

Date: _____

Work _____

Self _____

World _____

Date: _____

Work

_____

Self

_____

World

_____

Date: _____

Work

_____

Self

_____

World

_____

Date: _____

Work

_____

Self

_____

World

_____

Date: _____

Work

_____

Self

_____

World

_____

Date: _____

Work _____

Self _____

World _____

Overall Week's Gratitude

Work _____

Self _____

World _____

Date: _____

Work _____

Self _____

World _____

Date: _____

Work _____

Self _____

World _____

Date: _____

Work _____

Self _____

World _____

Date: _____

Work _____

Self _____

World _____

Date: _____

Work _____

Self _____

World _____

Date: _____

Work _____

Self _____

World _____

Date: _____

Work _____

Self _____

World _____

Overall Week's Gratitude

Work _____

Self _____

World _____

Date: _____

Work _____

Self _____

World _____

Date: _____

Work _____

Self _____

World _____

Date: _____

Work

_____

Self

_____

World

_____

Date: _____

Work

_____

Self

_____

World

_____

176

Date: _____

Work

_____

Self

_____

World

_____

Date: _____

Work

_____

Self

_____

World

_____

Date: _____

Work

_____

Self

_____

World

_____

Overall Week's Gratitude

Work

_____

Self

_____

World

_____

Date: _____

Work _____

Self _____

World _____

Date: _____

Work _____

Self _____

World _____

Date: _____

Work _____

Self _____

World _____

Date: _____

Work _____

Self _____

World _____

Date: _____

Work _____

Self _____

World _____

Date: _____

Work _____

Self _____

World _____

181

Date: _____

Work _____

Self _____

World _____

Overall Week's Gratitude

Work _____

Self _____

World _____

Date: _____

Work _____

Self _____

World _____

Date: _____

Work _____

Self _____

World _____

Date: _____

Work _____

Self _____

World _____

Date: _____

Work _____

Self _____

World _____

Date: _____

Work _____

Self _____

World _____

━━

Date: _____

Work _____

Self _____

World _____

Date: _____

Work

_____

Self

_____

World

_____

Overall Week's Gratitude

Work

_____

Self

_____

World

_____

Date: _____

Work

_____

Self

_____

World

_____

Date: _____

Work

_____

Self

_____

World

_____

Date: _____

Work

_____

Self

_____

World

_____

Date: _____

Work

_____

Self

_____

World

_____

Date: _____

Work
_____

Self
_____

World
_____

Date: _____

Work
_____

Self
_____

World
_____

Date: _____

Work _____

Self _____

World _____

Overall Week's Gratitude

Work _____

Self _____

World _____

Date: _____

Work

_____

Self

_____

World

_____

Date: _____

Work

_____

Self

_____

World

_____

Date: _____

Work _____

Self _____

World _____

Date: _____

Work _____

Self _____

World _____

Date: _____

Work
_____

Self
_____

World
_____

Date: _____

Work
_____

Self
_____

World
_____

Date: _____

Work _____

Self _____

World _____

Overall Week's Gratitude

Work _____

Self _____

World _____

Date: _____

Work
_____

Self
_____

World
_____

Date: _____

Work
_____

Self
_____

World
_____

Date: _____

Work

_____

Self

_____

World

_____

Date: _____

Work

_____

Self

_____

World

_____

Date: _____

Work

_____

Self

_____

World

_____

Date: _____

Work

_____

Self

_____

World

_____

Date: _____

Work _____

Self _____

World _____

Overall Week's Gratitude

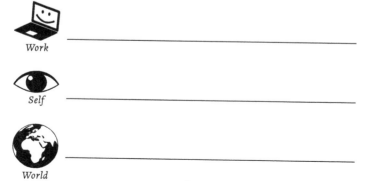

Work _____

Self _____

World _____

Date: _____

Work _____

Self _____

World _____

Date: _____

Work _____

Self _____

World _____

Date: _____

Work _____

Self _____

World _____

Date: _____

Work _____

Self _____

World _____

Date: _____

Work

_____

Self

_____

World

_____

Date: _____

Work

_____

Self

_____

World

Date: _____

Work

_____

Self

_____

World

_____

Overall Week's Gratitude

Work

_____

Self

_____

World

_____

Date: _____

Work

_____

Self

_____

World

_____

Date: _____

Work

_____

Self

_____

World

_____

Date: _____

Work _____

Self _____

World _____

Date: _____

Work _____

Self _____

World _____

Date: _____

Work

_____

Self

_____

World

_____

Date: _____

Work

_____

Self

_____

World

_____

Date: _____

Work _____

Self _____

World _____

Overall Week's Gratitude

Work _____

Self _____

World _____

Date: _____

Work _____

Self _____

World _____

Date: _____

Work _____

Self _____

World _____

Date: _____

Work

_____

Self

_____

World

_____

Date: _____

Work

_____

Self

_____

World

_____

Date: _____

Work
_____

Self
_____

World
_____

Date: _____

Work
_____

Self
_____

World
_____

Date: _____

Work
_____

Self
_____

World
_____

Overall Week's Gratitude

Work
_____

Self
_____

World
_____

Gratitude Monthly

All businesses and jobs depend on a vast number of
people, often unnoticed and unthanked, without
which nothing really gets done. They are all
human and deserve respect and gratitude.
Margaret Heffernan

Great entrepreneurs focus intensely on an
opportunity where others see nothing.
Naveen Jain

By reviewing a full month of your daily gratitude log, you may begin to notice patterns emerge or you may not see any. There is no right or wrong experience of looking back at the month.

You might, for example, discover that most of the items in The World category are from your garden. From this insight, you can make decisions — do you want to spend more time in your garden, or do you want to make a point of expanding the locations that inspire your gratitude?

In The Work section, you may see that this month your focus was on learning more than on acting. You might then ask yourself what the most important takeaways from the learning were and how you will put them to action. Or you may look over your month and be nourished by all the reasons you had to be grateful and more fully appreciate the life you are living.

Month: _____

Work

_____

Self

_____

World

_____

Month: _____

Work

_____

Self

_____

World

_____

Month: _____

Work _____

Self _____

World _____

Month: _____

Work _____

Self _____

World _____

Month: _____

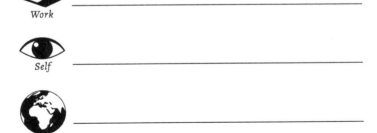

Work _____

Self _____

World _____

Month: _____

Work _____

Self _____

World _____

Month: _____

Work

_____

Self

_____

World

_____

Month: _____

Work

_____

Self

_____

World

Month: _____

Work

_____

Self

_____

World

_____

Month: _____

Work

_____

Self

_____

World

_____

Month: _____

Work

_____

Self

_____

World

_____

Month: _____

Work

_____

Self

_____

World

_____

Gratitude Quarterly

When we focus on our gratitude, the tide of disappointment goes out and the tide of love rushes in.
Kristin Armstrong

Real entrepreneurs have what I call the three Ps (and, trust me, none of them stands for 'permission'). Real entrepreneurs have a 'passion' for what they're doing, a 'problem' that needs to be solved, and a 'purpose' that drives them forward.
Michael Dell

Quarterly reviews and reports are standard in business. Quarters also roughly coincide with the four seasons in a year. Therefore, this is an important cycle to pay attention to in terms of your gratitude patterns and growth.

You have two options when looking back quarterly:

1. Skim every entry from the past ninety days.

2. Review your summaries by week or month or both.

Trust what you discover.

Quarter Months: _____

Work
_____

Self
_____

World
_____

Quarter Months: _____

Work
_____

Self
_____

World
_____

Quarter Months: _____

Work

_____

Self

_____

World

_____

Quarter Months: _____

Work

_____

Self

_____

World

Quarter Months: _____

Work _____

Self _____

World _____

Quarter Months: _____

Work _____

Self _____

World _____

Gratitude
Year in Review

*Gratitude makes sense of our past, brings peace
for today, and creates a vision for tomorrow.*
Melody Beattie

*At the age of 18, I made up my mind to never have
another bad day in my life. I dove into a endless
sea of gratitude from which I've never emerged.*
Patch Adams

Congratulations! You've completed a year of daily gratitude practice. You have achieved the gratitude habit. It will serve you for the rest of your life.

In the Year in Review pages of the journal, record your thoughts, ideas, and insights about your year of gratitude. How has it impacted your experience as a busy entrepreneur?

In the Year Ahead pages, write down your thoughts, ideas and goals for the coming year. Include both your gratitude goals and key business visions that your gratitude habit will support.

Year in Review

Year in Review

Year Ahead

Year Ahead

CPSIA information can be obtained
at www.ICGtesting.com
Printed in the USA
BVHW080554300821
615370BV00006B/16

9 780996 752435